TIFFANY'S
TABLE
MANNERS
—— FOR ——
TEENAGERS

TIFFANY'S
TABLE
MANNERS
— FOR —
TEENAGERS

By Walter Hoving

Drawings by Joe Eula

RANDOM HOUSE 🏠 NEW YORK

Visit us on the Web! www.randomhouse.com/teens

Educators and librarians, for a variety of teaching tools, visit us at
www.randomhouse.com/teachers

The Library of Congress has cataloged the previous edition of this work
as follows:
Hoving, Walter.   [Table manners for teenagers]
Tiffany's table manners for teenagers /
[text by Walter Hoving, drawings by Joe Eula].   p.   cm.
Originally published: Table manners for teenagers. New York: Washburn, 1961.
ISBN 978-0-394-82877-0 (trade)—ISBN 978-0-375-98308-5 (ebook)
1. Table etiquette—Juvenile literature.
I. Eula, Joe.   II. Tiffany and Company.   III. Title.
BJ2041.H68   1989   395'.54—dc19   88-23964

Printed in the United States of America
47 46 45 44 43 42 41 40 39

Foreword

GOOD MANNERS are as important as good grooming and good behavior. Unfortunately, however, in this day of confused standards, manners are sometimes sadly neglected. This is especially true of table manners.

At Tiffany's our interest in attractive tables set with good china, glass, and silverware makes us equally aware of the importance of good table manners.

But manners must not be stilted, self-conscious, or artificial. Therefore, it is dangerous to have one system, or no system, for home consumption and another for dining out. This is apt to cause dinner-table insecurity later in life.

So, training in table manners must be started early enough to make them automatic. Consequently we submit herewith our version of good table manners. There are other systems, and we don't quarrel with them, but we think this system is attractive, graceful, and above all, natural.

WALTER HOVING

Introduction

FIFTY YEARS AGO, after having lunch with me, my grandfather went home and wrote this book. To this day, I'm not sure what I did to inspire it, but I've always been very proud I played a role in its creation.

The year I was born he bought a struggling shop on Fifth Avenue. Using his intuitive knowledge that good design and a distinct point of view always translated to good business, he completely transformed Tiffany & Co. into a success story, and its blue box is recognized all over the world today.

Grandpa also gave Tiffany its direction and an authoritative voice that took positions and offered guidance, opinions, and lessons. His Tiffany newspaper ads defined good taste and design, and explored the meaning of the American goal, education, economics, and of course the need for good manners in everything we do.

He once said to me, "Johnny, it takes a person just as much effort to have bad manners as it does to have good manners, so why don't you take the time to learn some good ones?"

So I listened, and my manners must have improved, or I'm sure he would have written a sequel to this for adults.

JOHN HOVING

Contents

Let's Be Seated

It is customary for the young man to help the young lady on his right to be seated.

When you both have been seated, *don't* look around like a startled beetle. Turn directly to the young lady on your right and start talking.

First of all, let's get straight which fork or knife to use.

We like the method of placing the flat silver in the order of its use. You take the piece on the outside first.

Some people arrange the silver by size, so you have to learn to tell a fish knife from a meat knife and a fish fork from a meat fork. If there is no fish knife and fork, use the smaller knife and fork for the dish. If you make a mistake, just continue eating. *Don't* put the silver back on the table. Be nonchalant.

The place for the napkin is on the lap. Don't tie it around your neck or stick it in your belt.

The fish or meat will be served to you on your left side. Take the serving fork in your left hand and the serving spoon in your right, holding them as pictured above.

After you have served yourself, place the serving spoon and fork side by side on the platter.

Vegetables should also be placed on your plate. Side dishes, except for salads, are not used at home, only in restaurants.

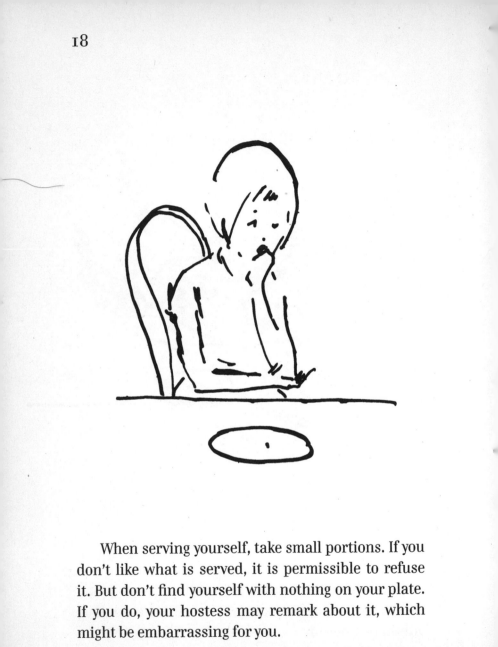

When serving yourself, take small portions. If you don't like what is served, it is permissible to refuse it. But don't find yourself with nothing on your plate. If you do, your hostess may remark about it, which might be embarrassing for you.

You don't have to wait for your hostess to start eating, but don't leap at your food like an Irish wolfhound.

The Soup Course

The soup is brought to the table in the soup plate at dinner.

The soup spoon is held in the right hand with the thumb on top.

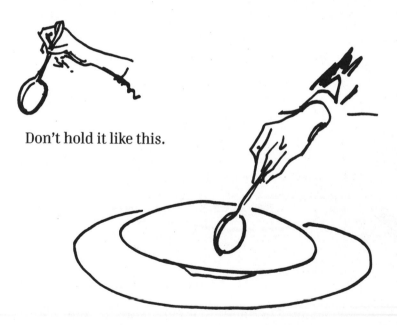

Don't hold it like this.

And don't hold it like a mashie niblick. This is not par for this course.

When you are eating soup, the soup spoon is tipped slightly away from you and is filled by moving it away from you, not toward you. Sip the soup from the side of the spoon or from the end—it makes no difference. And *please,* no noise.

When most of the soup is eaten, tip the soup plate away from you, never toward you. Thus, if you spill some, you will not splash your clothes.

Generally at luncheon soup is served in a cup. This may be eaten with a smaller soup spoon or drunk by lifting the cup.

The Fish Course

Both the fish knife and fork are used for the fish course.

This is the way to hold the fork. Prongs should *always* be down when the fork is held in the left hand.

This is the way to hold the knife. Note that it differs from the way the meat knife is held.

This is the way to place the fish on the fork. The fork is held in the left hand, and the knife is used to cut and as a pusher.

If the fish is soft and boneless, then it is perfectly proper to use only the fish fork. When the fork is held in the right hand, the prongs may be up or down, whichever is more convenient. When you are eating with the fork, don't put the knife on the plate. Leave it on the table. When using only the fork, *never* hold it in the left hand.

The Meat Course

The luncheon or dinner knives and forks are held this way.

The meat knife is not held like the fish knife because more leverage for cutting is necessary. Let the forefinger point down the handle.

And hold the fork in the left hand. The prongs are always pointed down.

You spear the meat with your fork and cut it off
with your knife. Cut only *one* piece at a time. To fix the
meat on the prongs of the fork, put the knife blade
underneath the piece of meat. A slight twist will help
to fix it firmly.

A small amount of potatoes and vegetables may be placed on the prongs of the fork with the meat.

The fork is conveyed to the mouth by twisting your wrist and raising your forearm slightly.

Don't stick your elbow out and raise your whole
arm like a derrick.

Each time you take a mouthful, lean over your plate. If anything drops, it will fall on the plate and not on your clothes.

After cutting the meat, never place the knife across the corner of the plate. Don't keep shifting the fork from the left to the right hand. This is clumsy and awkward.

Never hold the fork this way when cutting meat.

If occasionally you want to eat some vegetables with your right hand, place the knife as above. But do not shift the fork back and forth every time you cut a piece of meat.

Never hold the fork in the left hand with the prongs up and pile food on it with the knife.

Never hold the knife in the left hand.

While you are eating, *never* place the knife and fork like a pair of oars in a rowboat.

Always place them like this. This is the *only* "rest" position. The knife and fork are crossed on the plate with the fork over the knife with the prongs pointed down. This is one reason why the prongs are curved. A good butler or waitress will never remove your plate with the knife and fork crossed because he or she knows that you are not finished.

Never wipe your mouth with one hand while holding a knife or fork in the other.

Never keep the fork in the left hand while drinking water.

Do not hold the knife and fork in this position when you are talking. It looks unattractive and belligerent.

It is perfectly proper to talk with the knife and fork in your hands but do not gesticulate with the fork or the knife. The knife should *never* be raised more than an inch or two above the plate. If you remember this rule, you'll never get caught with the knife in your mouth.

When eating a piece of bread or drinking, place the knife and fork in the "rest" position. The sharp edge of the knife blade should be pointing to the left. This is the best place for your knife and fork when you are chewing, talking, or wiping your mouth.

When the course is finished, *always* place your knife and fork as above. The prongs of the fork should be down. The blade of the knife should face the fork. This is the "I am finished" position.

If the meat doesn't require cutting with the knife,
it may be eaten with the fork in the right hand. In this
case don't use the knife at all. Leave it on the table.

When eating only with the fork, place it, *prongs up,* on the plate when you are finished.

The butter knife is placed across the butter plate. Always break the bread with your fingers. Do not cut the bread with the butter knife; just butter the bread with it.

The Salad Course

The salad may be eaten with the salad knife and fork just as the fish and meat courses are eaten.

Or if you feel the salad can be cut with the edge of the salad fork, the knife may be left on the table.

At luncheon, salad is often served at the same time the meat course is served. In this case you may use the same fork you are using for the meat.

Asparagus is eaten with the fingers, unless stalks are too long.

If the asparagus is long and thin, cut off the ends with your fork held in your right hand and eat with your fork. You will then avoid imitating a trained seal. Then pick the shortened stalks up in your fingers.

An artichoke is eaten with the fingers. Pull off the leaves one at a time and draw them through your teeth. Don't try to swallow the whole leaf; it won't digest well.

When you get to the heart, use your knife and fork.

The Dessert Course

After the meat course the table is cleared of the dinner or luncheon plates and all unused silver. The peppers and salts are also removed, and the table is crumbed.

Then the dessert plate is served as above with the finger bowl, spoon, and fork on the plate.

Remove the finger bowl and place it on the table to the upper left of your plate.

Also remove the fork to the left and the spoon to the right. Do not leave the doily (if any) on your plate by mistake. It is not supposed to be eaten with your ice cream. This would alarm your hostess unduly.

The dessert may be eaten with the fork in the left hand (prongs down) and the spoon in the right. Eat with the spoon. The fork here serves only as a pusher.

If it is pie or cake, only the fork need be used; if ice cream or pudding, the spoon. The other piece is left on the table.

The same "rest" position of the fork and spoon is used as in the case of the knife and fork during the meat course. Place the fork prongs down, lying over the spoon.

This is the "I am finished" position of the fork and spoon: bowl up, prongs down.

If fresh fruit is served, another dessert or fruit plate is brought in with a fruit knife and fork on it. This is not often done in this country anymore, but it is quite common abroad. Take the apple or pear, quarter it with the fruit knife, and peel it. Then eat it, either with the fruit fork or with your fingers. Grapes are eaten with your fingers.

When it comes time to use your finger bowl, dip the tips of your fingers in it. But don't forget, it is not a bathtub; you're not supposed to dunk your whole hand. If you wish, you may also brush the tips of your wet fingers over your mouth. Then wipe your mouth, but don't let the water drip down your chin.

Some Don'ts . . .

Don't let your elbows stick out like flying buttresses. Keep them close to your sides.

Don't try to eat with your elbows on the table. It hampers your movements, and you may spill your food. Elbows should operate freely. You may, however, rest your elbows on the table when you're not eating.

Don't leave your spoon in your coffee cup.

Don't put too much in your mouth at once. It looks
as if you were brought up in a kennel.

Don't chew with your mouth open, and don't smack your lips. Not only is it unappetizing, but it interferes with other people's conversation.

Don't talk with your mouth full. Some of your lunch might fall out. You must learn, however, to talk with a little in your mouth, simply because you can't always wait until you have swallowed everything before answering a question. So if you take a little at a time, you will always be ready to join the conversation. This takes skill and practice.

When eating corn on the cob, hold it in both hands. Don't stick handles into each end as above. It looks too precious and artificial.

Don't eat chicken with your fingers except at a picnic. With a little practice you can dislodge enough chicken with your knife and fork to keep body and soul together till your next meal.

If you knock over your water glass, don't say, "Oops." Right the glass and keep talking to your partner. *Don't* start mopping the table with your napkin.

If you spill the water on your partner's dress, offer her your napkin and say you're sorry. But don't start mopping her. It might be misunderstood.

If you happen to drop your knife or fork on the floor *don't* dive down after it or peer down at it. Pick up another one and proceed according to plan.

Don't try to eat leaning back. It looks awful, and besides you will no doubt spill your food on your shirt.

Sit erect. Don't slouch.

If you find some gristle or a piece of meat you
cannot swallow, don't spit it out on your plate or into
your fist. Chew it into as small a piece as possible and
then place it on the prongs of your fork (or into your
spoon if the course calls for a spoon). Then place it on
the rim of your plate. Don't let this embarrass you. It
is perfectly correct. Olive pits or fish bones should be
removed with your fingers.

Don't throw your arm over the back of your chair.

Don't sit on the back of your neck.

Don't air your views in a loud voice.

Be more interested in hearing the other person's views than in expressing your own. That is the essence of good conversation.

When the table "turns," don't get left staring into space. Turn immediately to the girl on your left. If she doesn't turn to you, lean over and say something like this, "How about getting rid of that fascinating fellow on your left and paying a little attention to me?" Don't forget, faint heart never, etc., etc.

If you have to blow your nose don't be embarrassed. Just blow it. But use your *handkerchief,* not your napkin.

If perchance you inadvertently burp or your stomach rumbles, *don't* pat your stomach or your chest, or make any inane remarks about it.

Above all, *be natural. Don't* put on airs or try to be "backstairs refined" by sticking your finger out at a ninety-degree angle when you lift your cup to your mouth. And *don't* chew your food in a mincing, silly way. Just be yourself.

Don't push a plate away from you when you are through. Leave it where it is with the silverware properly placed.

Don't get up from the table until your hostess rises, and don't leave the dining room until your elders have left it.

So now that you know the rules you can start breaking them. Don't forget, though, it takes a lot of social know-how to break rules.

Remember that a dinner party is not a funeral, nor has your hostess invited you because she thinks you are in dire need of food. You're there to be entertaining. Be gay. Do your part. Don't be a gloom.

BON APPETIT!—